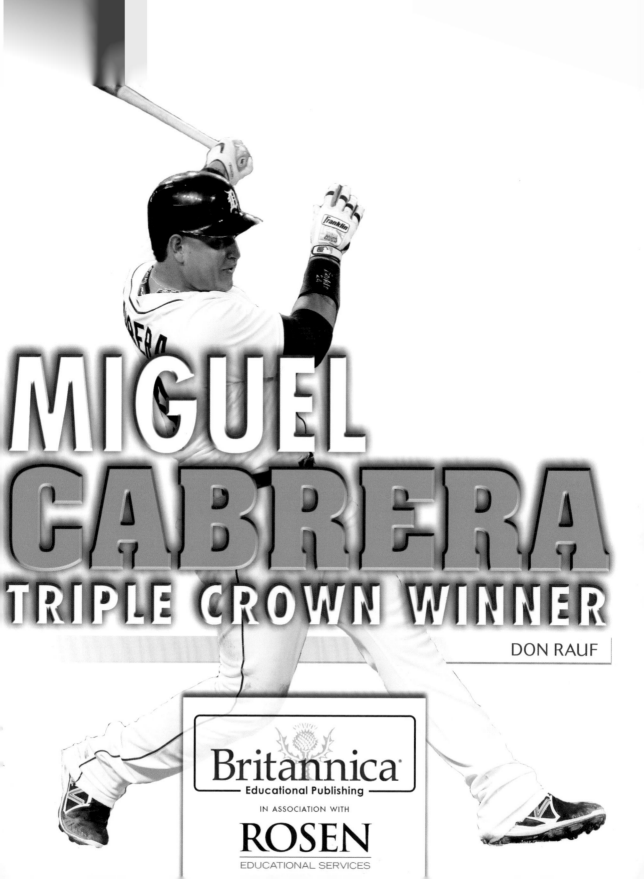

MIGUEL CABRERA
TRIPLE CROWN WINNER

DON RAUF

Britannica
Educational Publishing

IN ASSOCIATION WITH

ROSEN
EDUCATIONAL SERVICES

Published in 2016 by Britannica Educational Publishing (a trademark of Encyclopædia Britannica, Inc.) in association with The Rosen Publishing Group, Inc.

29 East 21st Street, New York, NY 10010

Distributed exclusively by Rosen Publishing.

To see additional Britannica Educational Publishing titles, go to rosenpublishing.com.

First Edition

Britannica Educational Publishing

J. E. Luebering: Director, Core Reference Group

Anthony L. Green: Editor, Compton's by Britannica

Rosen Publishing

Hope Lourie Killcoyne: Executive Editor

Nicholas Croce: Editor

Nelson Sá: Art Director

Nicole Russo: Designer

Cindy Reiman: Photography Manager

Library of Congress Cataloging-in-Publication Data

Rauf, Don, author.

Miguel Cabrera : triple crown winner/Don Rauf. — First edition.

          pages cm. — (Living legends of sports)

Includes bibliographical references and index.

ISBN 978-1-68048-094-8 (library bound) — ISBN 978-1-68048-095-5 (pbk.) — ISBN 978-1-68048-097-9 (6-pack)

1. Cabrera, Miguel, 1983– Juvenile literature. 2. Baseball players—Venezuela—Biography—Juvenile literature. I. Title.

GV865.C25R38 2016

796.357092--dc23

[B]

2014039769

Manufactured in the United States of America

CONTENTS

INNING	1	2	3	4	5	6	7	8	9	10	R	H
ISITOR	2	0	4	0	0	7	0	1	0	0	1 4	9
HOME	0	5	0	0	0	0	0	0	2	1	0 8	6

INTRO-
DUCTION

In many ways, Wednesday, October 3, 2012, wasn't an extraordinary day. In Kansas City, Missouri, the Detroit Tigers were playing a final game against the Kansas City Royals before the play-offs began. The Detroit Tigers had already clinched the title of American League Central champions. The team's star batter, Miguel Cabrera, was having a bad night. The Tigers' third baseman had flied out in the first inning and struck out in the fourth. It wasn't the best night for the league's best hitter.

Cabrera may have been distracted because on this night he was poised to become a Triple Crown winner. A Triple Crown winner is the rare batter who captures all three batting honors for the season for his league—most runs batted in (RBIs), best batting average, and most home runs.

Miguel "Miggy" Cabrera, of the Detroit Tigers, waves to the crowd in Kansas City on October 3, 2012, the day he became a Triple Crown-winning batter.

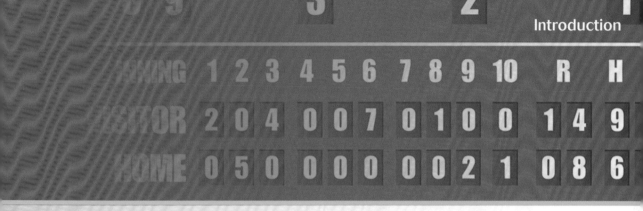

NING	1	2	3	4	5	6	7	8	9	10	R	H
TOR	2	0	4	0	0	7	0	1	0	0	14	9
HOME	0	5	0	0	0	0	0	0	2	1	0	8	6

The twenty-nine-year-old had the most RBIs—139. He also had the best batting average, .330. (This number represents the number of hits that puts a player on base per times at bat. Players with a batting average above .300 are considered very good.) Basically, Cabrera had been getting a base hit for every three times at bat.

He also had the most home runs for the season—forty-four. That was being threatened, though, in another game this night by New York Yankee center fielder Curtis Granderson.

Granderson started that game with a total of forty-one home runs for the season. But during the game, he hit one home run and then another. He was up to forty-three home runs. Cabrera saw that his shot at the title might slip away. Granderson, who was once Cabrera's teammate on the Tigers, was a dinger away from matching Cabrera's.

Granderson was due up to bat again in the seventh inning. With the Yankees way in the lead, Granderson gave up his turn at bat. When Cabrera heard the news, he knew the title was his.

Miguel Cabrera was the first to win the Triple Crown title in forty-five years, since Carl Yastrzemski won it in 1967. Miggy, as he was nicknamed, joined a list of some of the game's top sluggers, including Mickey Mantle, Ted Williams, and Lou Gehrig. The ballplayer who had started from humble beginnings in Venezuela had earned a spot among baseball's best and secured his spot in baseball history.

Baseball Was in His Blood

José Miguel Torres Cabrera was born on April 18, 1983, in Maracay, Venezuela. Miggy was raised in a small, dirt-floor home in a poor section of the city called Padrera. His home had one bathroom, a kitchen, and just two other rooms. It was one of five homes where he and his extended family lived. Although he grew up poor, Miggy didn't have to be rich to enjoy a supportive family and playing baseball. Sometimes, he would even play with a stick for a bat and a wad of paper as a ball.

From the very start, Cabrera seemed destined to play the game. Miggy's father—also named Miguel—was a good amateur ballplayer. When his plan to become a pro athlete didn't pan out, however, he became an auto mechanic.

Young baseball players stand in front of an advertisement featuring Cabrera. He is a hero in his home country of Venezuela.

For fourteen years, Cabrera's mother, Gregoria, played shortstop on the Venezuelan national softball team. Reportedly, his parents met on the baseball diamond—so when people say baseball was in Miggy's blood, it's true. When he was very small, he spent time playing in the dugout when his mom was busy snagging line drives in the field.

Baseball extended to his uncles as well. Uncle Jose Torres has operated a baseball training school in Maracay. His uncle David

Many in Cabrera's family played baseball, including his mother and father. His uncle Jose Torres has operated a baseball training school in his hometown.

Torres was signed to play in the St. Louis Cardinals system. He advanced to the minor leagues but his career petered out. Uncle David regularly helped train young Miggy. At age four, Cabrera was already tossing and hitting the ball.

QUICK FACT

Miggy grew up idolizing Dave Concepción, another baseball star from his hometown of Maracay. Concepción went on to be a top player with the Cincinnati Reds.

HOME 0 5 0 0 0 0 0 0 2 1 0 8 6 3

A Pro Ball Player in the Making

By age six, Miggy was highly competitive. All he could think about was playing in the big leagues. His uncle David would sometimes warn him to be cautious if he ever had the opportunity to play in North America. He didn't want his

Venezuelans love base-ball. Many young boys play the game with hopes of becoming as successful as Miguel Cabrera, and baseball scouts often go there to search for new talent.

nephew ever to be taken advantage of by any untrustworthy characters who might want to benefit from his talent and treat him unfairly. Uncle David wanted Miggy to protect himself.

When he was fourteen, Miggy had already grown into a physically solid and powerful hitter. He also had a strong right arm, rocketing off throws on target. He told his father that he really wanted to try to become a pro ballplayer. His father was glad that his son was so passionate about baseball, but he didn't want him to face the same disappointment that he had. He knew how hard it could be to achieve a career as a professional ballplayer. So his father encouraged him to keep after his dream but to have a backup plan and study engineering. He pushed Miggy and his sister to do well in school. He wouldn't support the baseball dream at all if he wasn't

QUICK FACT

Cabrera tapes his wrists when batting and writes *sangre* on the tape. In Spanish, *sangre* literally means "blood" but also means "family," and Cabrera says that is what he plays for.

HOME 0 5 0 0 0 0 0 0 2 1 0 8 6 3

Cabrera wanted to play with his dream team, the Florida Marlins. He liked many of the team's players, including shortstop Álex González .

keeping up his grades. When Cabrera wasn't swinging the bat, he was buried in his schoolbooks.

Hooked by the "Fish": Signing with the Marlins

The professional leagues from the United States are always keeping an eye out for budding talent. Reports of a young powerful slugger reached their offices. They sent scouts to check out the teen sensation Cabrera. Representatives from the Minnesota Twins, the Los Angeles Dodgers, and the New York Yankees were soon pacing the sidelines when Cabrera played. They were all amazed at this powerhouse at the plate.

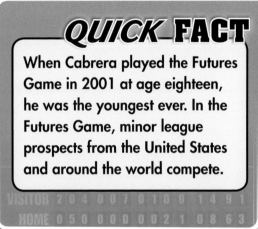

QUICK FACT

When Cabrera played the Futures Game in 2001 at age eighteen, he was the youngest ever. In the Futures Game, minor league prospects from the United States and around the world compete.

But Miggy liked one team in particular. He was a huge fan of the Florida Marlins. (They were nicknamed the "Fish" by some sportswriters). He admired several of the team's Latino players, including his countryman, shortstop Álex González. He rooted for the Marlins when they won the 1997 World Series, with help from Latino players Liván Hernández and Edgar Rentería.

After the Marlins' scout saw Cabrera in action, he got on the phone with Marlins management right away. He persuaded them to make Cabrera an offer to play for them immediately. The Dodgers and Yankees wooed him as well. The competition drove his offer price higher and higher.

For Cabrera, though, the Marlins were his dream team. More than any other team, the Marlins seemed to have a commitment to Hispanic players that Cabrera and his parents appreciated.

From Poor Young Boy to Millionaire Overnight

When the Marlins made an offer of $1.8 million, Cabrera jumped on it. He signed with the team on July 2, 1999. He was just sixteen years old. It was the highest amount ever paid for a Venezuelan prospect.

Reportedly, the short-tempered George Steinbrenner, the Yankees owner, blew his stack. When he lost the bid on Cabrera, he fired three of his scouts, as the story goes.

Cabrera was on his way to the big leagues. With a year to go before officially joining the Marlins, he kept in shape with Venezuela's Winter League, and he finished off his final year at Maracay High School.

Because Venezuela is in the Southern Hemisphere, the country has warm weather during the months between November and March. Teams in the Venezuelan Winter League compete with teams from the Dominican Republic, Mexico, Cuba, and Puerto Rico. The competition reaches a peak in February with the Caribbean World Series.

CHAPTER TWO

A Hot Prospect Hones His Game

Young Miggy would grow up to develop a powerful frame by the time he joined the Marlins. By age sixteen, he would stand 6 feet 2 inches (1.88 meters) tall and weigh in at about 185 pounds (83.9 kilograms). Because of his size, he would even be compared to one of the largest hitters in baseball history—Babe Ruth. In fact, Cabrera is bigger now. At the time of this writing, he weighed in at around 268 pounds (121.6 kg) while

When the Florida Marlins signed Cabrera, he was only sixteen years old. The young man, though, was bigger than his peers and had the makings of a power hitter.

Babe Ruth (who was also the same height as Cabrera) weighed 215 pounds (97.5 kg).

But Cabrera couldn't jump immediately to the big leagues. He had to put in his time in the minor leagues. Almost every major league player gets groomed in the minor leagues. Occasionally, baseball stars get drafted or signed to contracts and start in the major leagues—bypassing the minor league system entirely. (In recent times, pitcher Mike Leake was drafted by the Cincinnati Reds in 2009 after graduating from Arizona State and made his major league debut in 2010. Like Cabrera, some players went directly from high school to being signed by a professional team and a handful went directly from high school to major league play.)

QUICK FACT

Cabrera's career batting average is .320.

HOME 0 5 0 0 0 0 0 0 2 1 0 8 6 3

The Rookie Gets His Start

Cabrera, though, went right from high school to training in the minor leagues. In 2000, when he was seventeen, he started with the Gulf Coast League Marlins. This team was a rookie-level minor league affiliate of the Florida Marlins. The team played in Jupiter, Florida, at Roger Dean Stadium.

Cabrera started the same year as fellow Marlins Josh Beckett, Adrian Gonzalez, and Dontrelle Willis. They worked their way up the minor leagues together.

At this point, Cabrera wasn't quite the home run star he would turn into. He hit two home runs during his time with the Gulf Coast Marlins. Even so, players and fans alike recognized his talents. His batting average was .260, which was decent. This means that about every four times at bat he was getting a base hit. He knocked out ten doubles and two triples in fifty-seven games. His RBIs totaled twenty-two, and Cabrera himself ran in thirty-eight runs.

In the field, he was handling the position of shortstop well—stopping the balls and firing them off to first base.

Before he could play major league ball, Cabrera developed his skills with minor league teams, such as the New York Blue Sox (a Marlins affiliate team at the time).

Before the 2000 season ended, Marlins management decided to kick things up a notch for Cabrera. They sent him to the next level in the minor leagues. He joined the New York League Blue Sox (another Marlins affiliate team) in Utica, New York, for the final eight games of the season.

Cabrera kept his batting average about the same, at .250, and drove in six runs. Cabrera was being moved steadily along the system, and the Marlins were building a foundation for a strong player, easing him toward major league play.

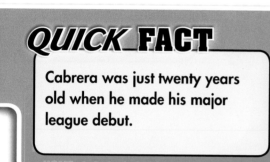

QUICK FACT

Cabrera was just twenty years old when he made his major league debut.

From Tigers to Cougars: Training Like the Big "Cats"

In the winter of 2000-2001, Cabrera headed back home to Venezuela to play in the Winter League there. For twenty-seven games, he played for the Aragua Tigers, a team that is part of the Venezuelan Professional Baseball League. (This wouldn't be the last time he played for a team called the Tigers.) The level of ball played by the Aragua Tigers has been compared to Triple A baseball, which is the highest level of play in minor league baseball. So for Cabrera, this was perfect training.

As the spring of 2001 came around, Marlins management sent Cabrera to play for the Kane County Cougars. Based in Geneva, Illinois, the Kane County Cougars are part of the Midwest League. In 2001, the team was affiliated with the Marlins but they went on to be affiliated with the Chicago Cubs. This was Class A minor league, a step up from the rookie level.

Cabrera steadily worked his way up through the minor leagues. He fine-tuned his htting while playing for the Kane County Cougars, based in Illinois.

Working Out His Weak Spots

Cabrera had a slow start in 2001. His game was in a slump during his first month with the Cougars. His hitting was down and his fielding was off. He made nineteen errors—meaning he made mistakes in the field that allowed the opposing team to advance on base.

Cabrera knew he needed to fix things. He sought help from Matt Winters, the team's hitting coach. Winters told Cabrera to adjust his stance at the plate. Cabrera tried standing taller. The coaching paid off. His batting average climbed to .279. He was running the bases with a new determination. His errors in the field dropped. The Marlins were seeing the dynamo they had signed regaining his confidence and stepping up his performance.

Cabrera was also becoming friends with first baseman Adrian Gonzalez. Cabrera still struggles with English, and having California-born Gonzalez as a pal gave him support.

QUICK FACT

Cabrera was the third player since 1900 to hit a game-winning home run in his first major league game.

First baseman Adrian Gonzalez also played for the Cougars. He became Cabrera's friend and gave him support as he adjusted to life in America.

Another Strong Season and a Move to Third Base

In the fall of 2001, Cabrera headed back to Venezuela for another winter season. He returned to the United States in the spring of 2002 and was back in Jupiter, Florida, where he started in the minor leagues. But this time he joined the Jupiter Hammerheads. The Hammerheads were part of the Florida State League and a Class A advanced affiliate team.

The Marlins moved Cabrera from shortstop to third base as they prepared him for major league ball. In 2003, with the Carolina Mudcats, his playing was better than ever.

The Marlins were still grooming him for the majors. They moved Cabrera from shortstop to third base. It took some adjustment, but he caught on quickly. By midseason, his batting average was still hovering at a strong .277 and he batted in forty-five runs. He wasn't a home run hitting star, but Cabrera was proving himself and moving forward. By the end of this season, he had homered only nine times with 489 times at the plate.

Increasingly, the Marlins were impressed and prepping Cabrera for a launch to the majors. They could tell that Cabrera was getting a strong feel for the strike zone.

Miggy's Breakout Season

The Marlins figured that after one more season of training, Cabrera would be in perfect shape for major league action. In the spring of 2003, Cabrera stepped into the baseball season with the Carolina Mudcats based in Zebulon, North Carolina.

For Cabrera, the season opened strong and just kept getting better. He became friends with a colorful pitcher on the team named Dontrelle Willis. Also known as the D Train, Willis wore his cap at a crooked angle and was known for his unusual pitching style, involving a high kick and an exaggerated body twist.

Cabrera was on fire. In April, his batting average soared to .402, and two months later it remained very high, at .365. He knocked out more home runs by June (ten homers) than he had his whole run in the minor leagues, and he had fifty-nine RBIs.

His minor league career had hit an all-time high. He couldn't wait to start with the majors the following year, but that opportunity came sooner than he expected.

A Leap to the Major Leagues

Miguel Cabrera was loving his time with the Mudcats. Word was spreading about the Venezuelan who was blasting out the hits. For the Marlins, however, the season was not going so well. On paper, the Marlins had one of the strongest teams in its history. Most of the players were top performers. They had won the World Series in 1997. But their performance on the field was sluggish in the first couple months of the season. They just couldn't seem to get things going. The Marlins head office decided to take some drastic measures. They fired the current manager and they called one of the most colorful managers in baseball out of retirement.

QUICK FACT

Cabrera won the American League's Most Valuable Player award two years in a row, in 2012 and 2013.

HOME 0 5 0 0 0 0 0 2 1 0 8 63

In 2003, the Marlins were struggling. To boost the team, they promoted Cabrera. In his debut, he hit a game-winning home run in the eleventh inning.

An Old Lion and a Young Buck Turn a Team Around

At age seventy-two, Jack McKeon became one of the oldest managers in professional baseball. He was not a coddler. He didn't believe in babying anyone or stroking egos. He was known to be tough and to get results, and that's exactly what happened.

To really ignite the team, however, the Marlins needed to do more. They decided to bring in new blood. The twenty-year-old Cabrera was moving on up to the big leagues—almost a year earlier than he had anticipated.

Besides making a leap to the majors, Cabrera had to make another adjustment. He had been playing third

QUICK FACT

Cabrera batted in 1,000 runs before his thirtieth birthday.

In 2003, the Marlins brought in a new "old" manager. Jack McKeon came out of retirement at age seventy-two and reignited the team.

base now for awhile. But the Marlins already had a stellar third base-man. So Cabrera was plugged into left field.

The shift required some retraining. The Marlins spent time with Cabrera showing him how to snag flies in the outfield, how to get into the right position against various hitters, and how to throw the ball to the right base fast and on target.

A Sensational Start from a Hot New Slugger

On June 20, 2003, Cabrera made his major league debut against the Tampa Bay Devil Rays. And it was dramatic. He came up empty in his first four at bats. In the bottom of the ninth inning, with two men on, he grounded out. At this stage, no one was expecting much from Cabrera. Even his father, who was listening to the game via the Internet, fell asleep.

When Cabrera's game slumped somewhat after his debut, he worked hard to improve it. His efforts paid off. He was named National League Rookie of the Month in July 2003.

Then, after the game had gone into extra innings, Cabrera cracked a home run straight down the middle of the field to win the game in the eleventh. Cabrera became the sixth-youngest player to homer in his first game.

His father woke up the next day and was astonished to hear the news. He ran to the local bodega and bought up all the newspapers. He was overjoyed at his son's winning hit.

His bat went a bit cold for the rest of June, but Cabrera was determined to turn that around. He worked on his hitting, and in July he came back with a vengeance. That month, his batting average was .318. He had five homers, eight doubles, and twenty-one runs batted in. For July, he was named the National League Rookie of the Month.

From Timid to Wild Card Contenders

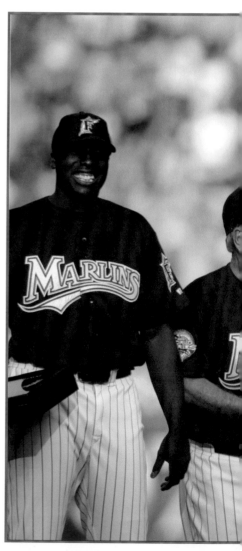

With Cabrera and manager McKeon helping to reignite the team, the Marlins had a shot at a wild card position in the play-offs in the fall.

In Major League Baseball in 2003, there was one wild card team from each league—one from the National League and one from the American League. This was the team with the best overall season record in the league after the three division winners. The divisions are East, West, and Central.

From 1994 to 2011, there was just one wild card team from each league. In 2012, a second wild card team was added to each league. So today, ten teams make the playoffs—five from the American League and five from the National League. The two wild cards are the two teams with the best records that do not win a division.

When third baseman Mike Lowell broke a bone in his left hand, it did not stop the winning Marlins. They did some fast reshuffling of positions, and Cabrera suddenly found himself back at third base. Cabrera mastered the new position. He always asked the more seasoned players a lot of questions and continually worked hard to improve his game.

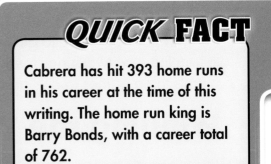

QUICK FACT

Cabrera has hit 393 home runs in his career at the time of this writing. The home run king is Barry Bonds, with a career total of 762.

Manager Jack McKeon (*center left*), Miguel Cabrera (*center*), and fellow Florida Marlin teammates acknowledge the fans after receiving their 2003 World Series Championship rings. The Marlins beat the Yankees, four games to two.

On September 26, the Marlins beat the New York Mets and clinched the wild card position. To get to the World Series, the Marlins would have to win the next two series for the league title. They beat the San Francisco Giants three games to one and then went on to face the Chicago Cubs.

Winning the World Series

Many people were rooting for the Cubs as "the lovable losers." The Cubs hadn't made it to the World Series since 1908, and it looked like they had a shot this year. The Cubs started strong and were up three games to one. Money was on the Cubs to win, but the Marlins charged back.

In the first inning of Game 4 of the 2003 World Series, Cabrera shined when he hit a home run off of star New York Yankee pitcher Roger Clemens.

In the tie-breaking seventh game, the Marlins flattened the Cubs with eight runs in the eighth inning before the stunned and dismayed crowd at Chicago's Wrigley Field.

The Marlins took the pennant for the National League and would face the mighty New York Yankees in the 2003 World Series. The Marlins were on fire and beat the Bronx Bombers, as the Yankees were known, in six games. Cabrera's shining moment came in Game Four with a homer off of star pitcher Roger Clemens. Within months, Cabrera had gone from minor league sensation to World Series winner.

CHAPTER
FOUR

A Superstar On and Off the Diamond

With a championship ring, Cabrera was now a baseball superstar. He was flooded with media attention and offers to endorse products. In Venezuela, he was a national hero and named Venezuelan Sportsman of the Year.

Some people attribute Cabrera's hitting success to a super sharp memory and attention to detail. He remembers how every pitcher throws, and he can often predict what's coming across the plate from closely watching the pitcher. That's why he says practicing with pitching machines is useless.

For the next four years after the Marlins World Series win, Cabrera remained a strong hitter all around but the Marlins just couldn't recreate the success they had in 2003. Cabrera stacked up impressive stats for home

QUICK FACT

Cabrera set a record as the highest-paid player when he signed a ten-year contract for $292 million.

HOME 0 5 0 0 0 0 0 2 1 0 8 6 3

runs, RBIs, and batting averages. At one point during these years, Cabrera's batting average reached an incredible .430.

Miggy Roars with the Detroit Tigers

In 2007 the Marlins decided they needed to reconstruct their team. They knew Cabrera was a great player, but they felt they could trade him and get new players to build a better, stronger team. So in 2007, Cabrera became a Detroit Tiger and started the 2008 season with them. He wound up with an eight-year deal worth $150 million. In 2011 the Tigers made it to the American League Championship but were shut down by the Texas Rangers.

In 2012 Cabrera not only found himself winning the Triple Crown, but also back in the World Series. The Tigers took on the San Francisco

Detroit welcomed Cabrera when he was traded to the Detroit Tigers in 2007. In 2014, Cabrera signed a record-breaking ten-year, $292 million contract with the team.

Giants but his team, which had shined all season, played poorly in the World Series. The Tigers gave up four games in a row to lose the series. Despite the disappointing loss, Cabrera's outstanding season earned him the American League's Most Valuable Player of the Year award.

In 2013 the Tigers again made it to the play-offs but missed a shot at the World Series when they lost to the Boston Red Sox. Although the Tigers did not make it to the play-offs in 2014, it was a big year for Cabrera and the team. At age thirty-one, Cabrera signed a contract extension with the Tigers worth $292 million.

Cabrera had certainly come a long way from the streets of Venezuela. While on his phenomenal rise, he always held his home and family close to his heart.

QUICK FACT

Cabrera was the American League batting champion three years in a row in 2011, 2012, and 2013. He had the best batting average in the league during those three years.

HOME 0 5 0 0 0 0 0 2 1 0 0 6 3

Married with Children

Back in 2002, he married his childhood sweetheart Rosangel. He met her when she was thirteen. When they dated, they often went to the movies. Miguel and Rosangel

Miguel Cabrera married his childhood sweetheart, Rosangel. They started dating when she was thirteen years old. They now have two daughters and a son—Brisel, Isabella, and Christopher.

both love to watch movies together to this day. The couple currently lives in Michigan with their two daughters and one son. Their names are Rosangel (nicknamed Brisel), Isabella, and Christopher. Every chance he gets, Cabrera takes his kids to one of his favorite places in America—Disney World. The family also has a Yorkshire terrier named La Cosita, which means "little thing." He and Rosangel renewed their marriage vows after the 2003 World Series.

Cabrera believes in using his money and fame to help others. Here in 2012 he attended a benefit to cure paralysis. He follows this motto: "Work hard. Dream big. Help others."

Many say that Cabrera is a mystery because he doesn't reveal much about himself. He is known as a man of few words around strangers. To friends, he's a warm and friendly guy, but it takes him a while to open up to people. Some people suspect that he still feels like a stranger in a strange land in the United States and that he's not comfortable in the spotlight. Teammates have described him as fun loving, serious about baseball, dedicated to family, and terrific with children.

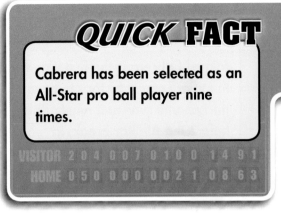

QUICK FACT

Cabrera has been selected as an All-Star pro ball player nine times.

Cabrera enjoys archery as a hobby. He finds it relaxing. He tried golf but a good bat swing didn't translate into a good golf swing, so he gave it up.

Helping Others Reach Their Dreams

Now that Cabrera is hugely successful, he believes in giving back and helping the world be a better place. He founded the Miguel Cabrera Foundation to help kids and families thrive using baseball as a path to reach their goals. The foundation's mission is to undertake youth development programs, community ballpark makeovers, and establish youth leadership academies in the United States, throughout Latin America, and in the Caribbean. His foundation awards college scholarships, too.

Never Forgetting Where He Came From

Cabrera always remembers his Venezuelan roots. He continues to go back to Venezuela to see family, friends, and people in the community. When he returns, he likes to eat at the restaurant Weekend Burger and

QUICK FACT

Miguel Cabrera is the first player in Major League history to have thirty home runs and ninety RBIs before the All-Star break, in mid-July.

HOME 0 5 0 0 0 0 0 0 2 1 0 8 6 3

watch telenovelas (soap operas). His favorite telenovela is *Cosita Rica* ("Little Rich Thing").

As the awards for his athletic ability kept flooding in over the years, Cabrera never lost sight of his pride in being Venezuelan.

"For as long as I can remember, playing baseball has been my life. That's why I don't lose sleep over winning prizes," Cabrera

Cabrera established a foundation to help kids thrive by using baseball as a path to reach their goals. Throughout his career, he has maintained his pride in being Venezuelan.

said in a speech after receiving an award given to the best Venezuelan major league player of the year in 2012.

"If I win them, that's fine, but what I think about first of all is my responsibility. I value prizes as a nice memory to share with my family, with my grandchildren when I'm old, and for the happiness it brings to all Venezuelans."

Children in Venezuela idolize him and welcome his visits. Cabrera's foundation just helped renovate a field in his native Maracay but also has targeted locations in Detroit and Miami, his offseason home.

Cabrera continues to live by the motto of his foundation: "Work hard. Dream big. Help others." And he continues to inspire people to do just that.

TIMELINE

April 18, 1983: Miguel Cabrera is born in Maracay, Venezuela.

July 2, 1999: Signs with the Florida (now Miami) Marlins for $1.8 million.

June 20, 2003: Makes major league debut against the Tampa Bay Devil Rays. Hits game-winning home run.

October 22, 2003: Hits first-inning home run off legendary Yankee pitcher Roger Clemens, setting tone for a World Series Game Four victory.

October 25, 2003: Celebrates World Series win over New York Yankees.

December 5, 2007: Traded to the Detroit Tigers.

July 22, 2012: Hits 300th career home run.

October 3, 2012: Wins Major League Baseball's Triple Crown.

October 24, 2012: Plays in his second World Series. The Tigers lose in a four-game sweep to the San Francisco Giants.

November 15, 2012: Named Most Valuable Player in the American League.

November 14, 2013: Named Most Valuable Player in the American League for the second time.

March 27, 2014: Agrees to a record-breaking contract extension with the Detroit Tigers worth $292 million.

April 4, 2014: Cabrera gets his 2,000th career hit.

OTHER LIVING LEGENDS OF BASEBALL

Ichiro Suzuki (1973–) An outfielder for the Yankees since 2012, Ichiro played with the Seattle Mariners for eleven years. He holds a number of records, including most hits in a single season of Major League Baseball—262. He has had ten consecutive seasons with at least 200 hits, the longest streak by any player in history.

Derek Jeter (1974–) Before retiring at the end of the 2014 season, he played shortstop for the New York Yankees for twenty seasons and was captain of the team from 2003 on. His performance helped the Yankees win the World Series in 1996, 1998, 1999, and 2000.

David Ortiz (1975–) Nicknamed Big Papi, Ortiz is a nine-time All Star and a three-time World Series champion. He holds the single-season record for the Red Sox for home runs. He hit fifty-four during the 2006 season.

Jose Bautista (1980–) An outfielder for the Toronto Blue Jays, he led the major league in home runs in 2010 and 2011. He has appeared in four All-Star Games. He has won two Hank Aaron Awards, given each year to the top hitter in each league.

Albert Pujols (1980–) The first baseman for the Los Angeles Angels, Pujols is the only player in major league history to have a batting average of at least .300 with at least thirty home runs and one hundred runs batted in (RBIs) in his first 10 seasons.

Robinson Canó (1982–) The second baseman for the Seattle Mariners, he was part of the 2009 Yankees World Series championship team. He has been chosen as a major league All-Star six times. He has ranked in the top ten among American League players for hits, at bats, doubles, batting average, runs scored, and triples.

Justin Verlander (1983–) A star pitcher for the Detroit Tigers, he has pitched two career no-hitters. In 2011, he received the American League Cy Young Award, an annual prize given to the outstanding pitcher in both of the two major leagues.

Buster Posey (1987–) The catcher for the San Francisco Giants, he has been a World Series champion twice. He's also been an All-Star twice and National League batting champion and Most Valuable Player in 2012.

Mike Trout (1991–) Nicknamed the Millville Meteor, the twenty-three-year-old debuted in 2011 and had an amazing season in 2012, winning the American League Rookie of the Year Award, the Silver Slugger Award, and finishing as runner-up to Miguel Cabrera for Most Valuable Player that year. He was a legendary rookie who led the league in runs scored and stolen bases in his debut year.

GLOSSARY

ball A pitch that does not enter the strike zone and is not hit by the batter. If a pitcher delivers four balls, the batter walks to first and is on base. Sometimes, a pitcher will walk a strong batter on purpose.

batting average A number that shows how often a batter gets a base hit.

dynamo Someone who has a lot of energy.

error A mistake made by a player while playing baseball.

inning One of the usually nine parts of a baseball game in which each team bats until three outs are made.

Major League Baseball The professional baseball organization in the United States. It is organized into two leagues—the American League and the National League. There are fifteen teams and three divisions in each league.

minor leagues A collection of professional baseball teams in the United States that compete at levels below the Major Baseball League level. Minor league teams are affiliated with major league teams and used as a training ground for major league players.

pennant The prize that is awarded to the champions of the American League and the National League each year or the championship itself.

RBI Run batted in. A common statistic used to define how good a batter is.

shortstop The player who defends the area between second and third base.

strike zone The area over home plate through which a pitched baseball must pass to be called a strike. If the umpire rules a pitch is out of the strike zone, it is a ball.

wild card As of 2012, the two teams in each league with

the best record among the non-division-winning teams.
From 1994 until 2012, there was only one wild card team for each league.

wrist taping Batters tape their wrists to help prevent injuries from twisting. The taping helps prevent too much movement.

FOR MORE INFORMATION

Books

Chandler, Matt. *Side-by-Side Baseball Stars: Comparing Pro Baseball's Greatest Players.* North Mankato, MN: Capstone Press, 2014.

Detroit Free Press. *Days of Roar!: From Miguel Cabrera's Triple Crown to a Dynasty in the Making!* Detroit, MI: Detroit Free Press: 2013.

Doeden, Matt, with contributor Matt Scheff. *Miguel Cabrera: Baseball Superstar* (Sports Illustrated Kids: Superstar Athletes). North Mankato, MN: Capstone Press, 2014.

Fishman, Jon. *Miguel Cabrera* (Amazing Athletes). Minneapolis, MN: Lerner Publishing Group, 2013.

Mattern, Joanne. *Miguel Cabrera* (Robbie Readers: Biographies). Newark, DE: Mitchell Lane Pub Inc, 2013.

Websites

Because of the changing nature of Internet links, Rosen Publishing has developed an online list of websites related to the subject of this book. This site is updated regularly. Please use this link to access the list:

http://www.rosenlinks.com/LLS/Cab

INDEX